practice pad
grammar

Using this book

This **Smart Start Practice Pad** is designed to support and consolidate the grammar skills your child will be taught in school. Practising these key skills is important but at the same time learning should be fun. Here are some useful tips:

✪ Start at the beginning of the book and explain to your child how to complete each exercise.

✪ Always praise your child's efforts. They may not always get it right first time, but use the answers in the back of the book to check their work, and to help them to understand and correct any errors.

✪ Make up games to make their learning fun. Find nouns in the house, or act out verbs.

✪ Point out some of their learning in their storybooks during shared reading. Try finding plurals, or high five every time they spot a conjunction.

✪ These exercises cover a range of topics and abilities, so don't worry if your child finds them too challenging – just try again at a later stage.

✪ Tear out the pages to display your child's work, or laminate them first to use with dry-wipe pens so your child can practise and perfect their skills.

✪ Use the stickers at the back of the book as a motivational reward for completing the exercises.

picthall and gunzi

an imprint of Award Publications Limited

Naming nouns

A word for a person, a place or a thing is called a **noun**. Draw a line from each of these nouns to the matching picture.

fish

book

tractor

farm

horse

firefighter

house

dog

Place your sticker here

A B C D E F G H I J K L M N O P Q R S T U V W X Y Z

Capital letters and full stops

When we write a sentence, we put a **capital letter** at the start and a **full stop** at the end. We also use capital letters for proper nouns, titles and for 'I'.

> **Proper nouns are names of:**
> places (e.g. countries, towns), people and animals (e.g. pets), days of the week and months of the year.

Rewrite these sentences with capital letters and full stops in the correct places.

i have a Pet hamster called squeak

my Cousin ryan lives in canada

daisy and zoe are going to a Party On saturday

i'm Learning to Play the guitar

Place your sticker here

Muddled sentences

The words in these sentences are in a muddle! Write the words in the correct order to make the sentences make sense!

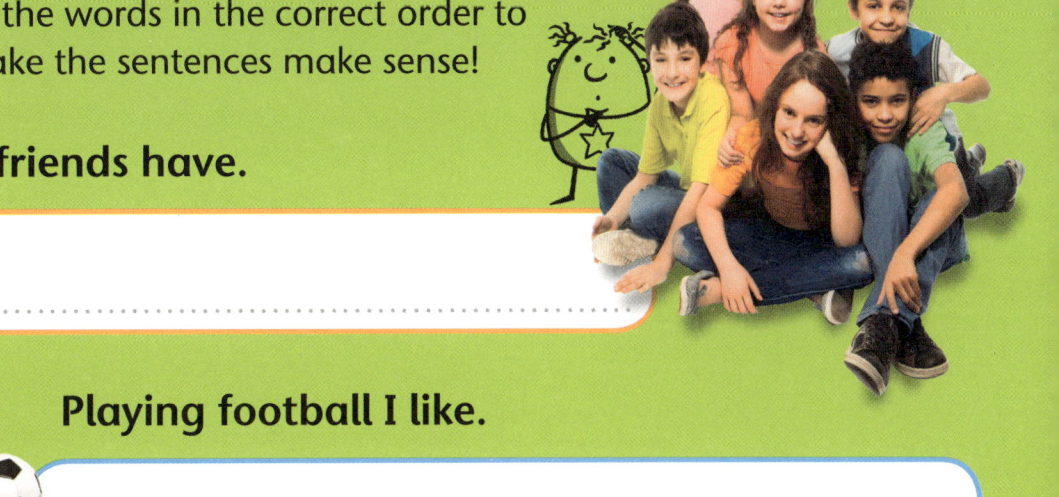

I lots of friends have.

Playing football I like.

My dog is Bobby called.

I getting up in the don't like morning.

My April birthday is in.

Place your sticker here

Determiners

Determiners are words that come before a noun to make it clear which thing we are referring to and who owns it. They can also show quantities or amounts.

Find the nouns below then underline the **determiners**, as shown.

"There are <u>lots of</u> animals at the zoo."
"Look at those monkeys in the tree."
"One monkey just took my banana!"
"Which monkey? This monkey?"
"No, that monkey! I will eat some grapes instead."

When a noun starts with a **vowel** (a, e, i, o, u) we use 'an'.

When a noun starts with a **consonant** (**c**at, **b**ook, **g**uitar) or a vowel that is pronounced like a consonant (e.g. 'one' sounds like it begins with a 'w', and 'unit' sounds like it begins with a 'y') we use 'a' before it.

Write '**an**' or '**a**' as the correct determiner for these words.

☐	elephant	☐	orange
☐	aeroplane	☐	hour
☐	dragon	☐	house
☐	eagle	☐	unicorn

Note: There are some exceptions. H is tricky, as it depends on whether the sound is **hard** or **soft**. If it is a soft *h*, we use *an* (e.g. *an hour*). For a hard *h*, we use *a* (e.g. *a house*).

Check your answers. Did you get these two right?

Adding adjectives

Describing words are called **adjectives**. They tell us more about nouns. Circle the correct adjective to describe each picture.

A **blue** / **yellow** fish

A **stripy** / **spotty** ball

A **green** / **red** apple

A **slow** / **fast** car

A **tall** / **short** sunflower

A **little** / **big** dog

Can you think of any more adjectives to describe the people and objects in these pictures?

Place your sticker here

Choosing adjectives

Join an **adjective** from the left to a **noun** on the right.
Use each word once and make sure they make sense together.

delicious	party
sandy	sky
fun	meal
difficult	tree
blue	beach
tall	sum

Write your own **adjectives** to describe these **nouns**.
Circle **a** or **an** in front of each one to match the adjective you used.

a/an .... ice cream

a/an .... car

a/an .... shark

Place your sticker here

Expanding noun phrases

A phrase is part of a sentence that does not have a verb.

1 A fish

This is a noun phrase.
It cannot be a sentence because it does not have a verb.
We can expand it and make it more informative
and interesting by adding adjectives.

2 An orange fish

3 An orange, stripy fish

or

An orange fish with white stripes

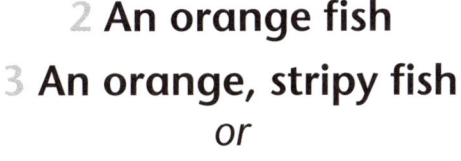

For each of the objects below, write two expanded noun phrases.

1 An umbrella

2 ....

3 ....

1 The racing car

2 ....

3 ....

1 A present

2 ....

3 ....

Place your sticker here

Vital verbs

A sentence must have a **verb**.
Without one, it is a phrase.
Verbs are **doing** or **being** words.

What is happening in these pictures?
Circle the verbs.

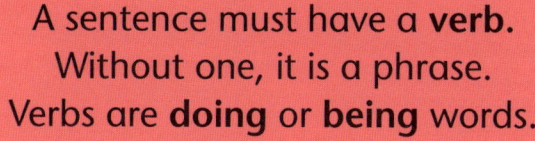

The boy plays with the train.

The boy in the green t-shirt jumps up high.

The girl with bunches clapped her hands.

The girl drew with her coloured pencils.

Place your sticker here

Past tense verbs

The verbs in a sentence tell us when something is happening – whether it is happening **now** or happened in the **past**.
Often, the letters 'ed' are added to the end of a verb to show an event happened in the past. This type of verb is called a **regular verb**.

For example:
I jump. ▶ This is happening **now**.
I jump**ed**. ▶ This happened in the **past**.

Rewrite these sentences to show they happened in the past.

I <u>climb</u> up a steep mountain last weekend.

....

I <u>play</u> tennis with my friends every day last week.

....

Last year, I <u>act</u> in the school play.

....

Yesterday, I <u>finish</u> my homework then <u>watch</u> TV.

....

Place your sticker here

Past tense verbs

The verbs in a sentence tell us when something is happening — whether it happened now or happened in the past. Often the letters 'ed' are added to the end of a verb to show it happened in the past. This type of verb is called a regular verb.

Examples:
jump → This is jumping.

More past tense verbs

Some verbs are **irregular** because they do not follow the regular rule of adding 'ed' to the end to create the simple past tense. Often this is because adding 'ed' sounds peculiar or is difficult to say.

> **For example:**
> I **go** to the cinema. ▶ I **went** to the cinema.
> They **do** well at school. ▶ They **did** well at school.

Draw lines to join the present tense verbs on the left to their past tense forms on the right.

Happening now   Has already happened

cry   drew

swim   bought

think   stood

buy   wrote

go   cried

draw   caught

write   swam

see   thought

catch   went

stand   saw

Place your sticker here

Using adverbs

An **adverb** describes or tells us more about a **verb**.
They usually end in **ly** but not always.
Circle the adverbs in the passage below.
The verbs have been underlined to help you.

I <u>ran</u> faster. My heart <u>beat</u> rapidly. The others were quickly <u>catching</u> up. As I <u>crossed</u> over the finish line, the crowd <u>cheered</u> wildly. I proudly <u>took</u> first place.

(Notice how the writing still makes sense if you remove the adverbs.)

Adverbs tell us **how, when, where, how often (frequency)**, or **how much (degree)** something is done. Choose an adverb from below to complete each of the sentences

How	When	Where	Frequency	Degree
loudly	early	away	always	probably

The mouse ran .... from the cat.

The children shouted ....

He arrived .... at school.

I will .... go to the party.

She .... danced when she was happy.

Place your sticker here

Word beginnings

We can change the meaning of a word by adding a '**prefix**' at the beginning. For example, we can change **kind** to **unkind** by adding '**un**'.

Choose the correct prefix to complete the words below.

un = not
re = again
dis = not, opposite of

well .... well tidy .... tidy

load .... load like .... like

wrap .... wrap fill .... fill

Challenge:
Can you think of any other words that use the prefixes **un**, **dis** or **re**?

Place your sticker here

Word families

Words belong to **families**. Some words share sounds (such as d**own**, fr**own**, br**own**). Others share a root word, whose meaning is changed by prefixes and/or suffixes.

> **For example:**
> *happy* – **happi**ness, un**happy**
> *help* – un**help**ful, **help**er

Choose a word from the ones in the coloured ovals below to complete each of these sentences and underline the root word in the **bold** words.

- climbing
- painter
- useless
- teacher
- acting
- drove

The .... **painted** the house.

The **driver** .... the bus.

The **climber** is .... a mountain.

The .... is **teaching** her class.

I **used** the eraser, but it was ....

The **actor** is .... in a play.

Can you think of any other word families?

Place your sticker here

Prepositions

A **preposition** tells us when or where something is, or when or where it happened.
Think pre**POSITION** to help you remember.

> **For example:**
> They played chase *during* playtime. (when)
> I sat *next to* my friend. (where)

Underline the prepositions in the sentences below.

She played on the swings.

May is between April and June.

We jumped into the puddle.

I will read until it's time for bed.

Below is a list of prepositions. Can you match each preposition with its opposite (or antonym)?

before ········· in
up   after
out   over
under   down

Place your sticker here

Personal pronouns

When we want to avoid repeating a noun, we use a **pronoun**. This makes our writing flow more smoothly.

For example:

I spotted a rare butterfly. But the butterfly flew away before I could take a photo of the butterfly.
The word '**butterfly**' is repeated.

I spotted a rare butterfly. But it flew away before I could take a photo of it.
We can use '**it**' to replace the word '**butterfly**'.

Choose **pronouns** from the list below to fill in the gaps in these sentences.

he   she   him   her   they   them   it   I

I saw Jack today. .... invited .... to my party.

I hope .... can come. Amy is invited too,

but it is .... sister's birthday on the same day.

Do you think .... will come?

I didn't tell either of .... about the magic show.

.... will be awesome! .... will love it.

Place your sticker here

Possessive pronouns

We use **possessive pronouns** to show who owns something.

For example:

my bag   his bag   her bag   their bags   our bags   your bag

Underline the **possessive pronouns** in the sentences below.

Is this <u>your</u> hat? It's just like <u>mine</u>!

My team is in red and hers is in blue.

His dog is a terrier and mine is a poodle.

My favourite number is 5. What's yours?

Our t-shirts are the same, but theirs are different.

Their team lost and our team won.

I've got my ticket. Have you got yours?

Place your sticker here

Helping Verbs

The verb 'to be' has many forms. For example:
'am', **'is'** and **'was'** for one person or thing.
'are' and **'were'** for more than one person or thing.

It is a helping (auxiliary) verb that is used to show **when** another verb happened.

Circle the correct auxiliary verb to complete the sentences below.

The parrot is/are squawking.

The balloons is/are floating.

We was/were jumping.

They was/were swimming.

She was/were eating.

The children is/are playing.

The sheep was/were in their field.

The fish is/are swimming in its tank.

Using the verb 'to be' as an auxiliary verb:
Past: was/were being
has/have/had been
Present: am/is/are being
Future: will be

Place your sticker here

Bossy Verbs

Modal verbs (sometimes known as 'bossy verbs') show us a command, ability, possibility or give advice. It is important to choose the correct **modal verb** to give your sentence the correct meaning.

For example, see how the meaning of this sentence changes:
You **can** go to the toilet. (You are able to.)
You **may** go to the toilet. (You have permission to.)
You **could** go to the toilet. (You have the opportunity to.)
You **should** go to the toilet. (You are being advised to.)
You **must** go to the toilet. (You are being told to, or it is necessary to.)

Modal verbs are:

can	shall	will	got to
could	should	would	need to
may	ought	must	have to
might			

Write some sentences of your own using modal verbs.

....
....
....
....

Place your sticker here

Making a sentence

Most sentences have at least one **subject** (the 'doer', which is usually a noun or a pronoun) and one **verb** (the 'doing' word).

> **Meat-eating <u>dinosaurs</u>. Are carnivores.**   ✘ wrong
> These are incomplete sentences because the verb (are) and subject (dinosaurs) are split up by the full stop.
> **Meat-eating dinosaurs are carnivores.**   ✔ right

Put a tick (✔) or a cross (✘) against each of the examples below, then circle the verb and underline the subject in each sentence.

- ☐ Many dinosaurs. Ate only plants.
- ☐ Many dinosaurs ate only plants.

- ☐ Tyrannosaurus rex had a massive bite.
- ☐ Tyrannosaurus rex had a. Massive bite.

- ☐ Some of the biggest dinosaurs. Had the smallest brains.
- ☐ Some of the biggest dinosaurs had the smallest brains.

Place your sticker here

Compound sentences

An **independent** (or main) **clause** makes sense on its own. It is a **simple sentence**. When two or three are joined by a connecting word, it creates a **compound sentence**. Choose a connecting word from the box to complete each of the sentences below.

> for   and   nor   but   or   yet   so

I wore a hat ....*for*.... it was a sunny day.

I ate too much ice cream .... I felt sick.

She wanted to say hello .... she was too nervous.

I sprained my elbow .... my arm was put in a sling.

You can either go to the pool .... the cinema.

Fish have neither feet .... hands.

He dislikes the sand .... he is at the beach.

The meaning of a sentence can change if you use a different joining word.
For example, which of the two sentences would you rather hear?

You can go out to play, but do your homework first.

You can go out to play or do your homework first.

Place your sticker here

Short and sweet

A sentence should be made up of one or two pieces of information. These are called **clauses**. Any more than this and your writing may become confusing and difficult to understand.

Cross out '**and**' where you can make a new sentence, then put in a full stop. Remember to start each new sentence with a capital letter.

Dear Ollie,

We are having a great time in Silver Bay and the weather has been hot and sunny every day and we went to the beach yesterday and Charlie and I had a surfing lesson and it was awesome and I hope you are enjoying your holiday and see you back at school next week.

Emily x

Place your sticker here

Complex sentences

Complex sentences are made up of an **independent** (main) **clause** (which makes sense on its own) and a **dependent** (subordinate) **clause** (which gives more information but does not make sense on its own). Notice that when the subordinate clause comes first, a comma separates it from the main clause.

For example:

We can go to the park after we've had lunch.
Main clause (makes sense on its own) — Subordinate clause (does not make sense on its own)

After we've had lunch, we can go to the park.
Subordinate clause — Main clause

Decide which are main and which are subordinate clauses. Then see if you can match them to make complete sentences. Remember to include the correct punctuation.

I saw a lion	because I was cold
I must brush my teeth	I wore my coat
if you teach them	before I go to bed
some parrots can talk	I feel so strong
	when I went to the zoo
	since I took up karate

Place your sticker here

Sentence functions

The sentences we write have jobs to do. Choosing the correct words – and punctuation – is important to make our meaning clearly understood.

The four functions are:

Commands
give us instructions or orders.

Questions
ask for information or permission.

Statements
give us facts and information.

Exclamations
start with 'what' or 'how' and express emotion.

Read the sentences below and decide what their function is. Write a 'C', 'Q', 'S' or 'E' in the box to show your answer.

☐ Take the dog for a walk.

☐ How marvellous!

☐ Where do you live?

☐ Please post the letter.

☐ My birthday is next month.

☐ What beautiful birds!

☐ You're my best friend.

☐ Will you tidy your room, please?

Place your sticker here

Using speech marks

We use **speech marks** to show words that are spoken. We use one (an opening speech mark) before the first spoken word, and another (a closing speech mark) after the punctuation following the last word that is spoken.

> My new computer game is called Monster Mash.
> Do you want to play it? "Jess asked Omar." ✗ wrong
>
> "My new computer game is called Monster Mash.
> Do you want to play it?" Jess asked Omar. ✓ right

Continue reading the story below.
Put in speech marks around the things Omar and Jess say.

I can't. I've hurt my finger, replied Omar.

He showed Jess the plaster covering his finger.

How did you do that? asked Jess.

A monster bit me the last time I played! replied Omar.

Ha, ha! Very funny! laughed Jess.

Note: speech bubbles don't need speech marks.

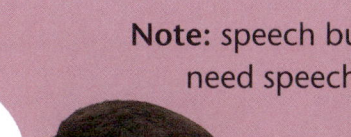

A monster bit me the last time I played!

Ha, ha! Very funny!

Place your sticker here

Using commas

Commas can be used to separate lists of words in a sentence. They help the sentence to make sense.

I like swimming dogs, reading and painting.   ✗ wrong

I like swimming, dogs, reading and painting.   ✓ right

Now we know you like dogs *and* swimming, rather than dogs that can swim. Notice there is no comma before the last item in the list, instead the word **'and'** has been used.

Tip: If you can replace the comma with **and** or **or**, you know it's correct.

Use the examples above to help you insert five missing commas into the story below.

It was a warm sunny day. Mum asked Connor to go to buy jam flour butter and eggs so that they could make a delicious cake for Grandma. Connor wondered if he should cycle walk or run through the dark spooky forest to get to the shops.

Place your sticker here

Commas for sense

We also use commas to make our writing clear. Without them, we might not understand what is meant.

Let's eat Grandma.   ✗ wrong
Let's eat, Grandma.   ✓ right

This tells Grandma it's time to eat, rather than that we should eat Grandma!

Sometimes, one comma is used, like in the example above. Sometimes, two or more commas are needed.

My ball like a kite soars through the air.   ✗ wrong
My ball, like a kite, soars through the air.   ✓ right

The commas make us pause and show the balloon is being compared to a kite.

The sentences below could be misunderstood. In total, 7 commas are missing. Can you place them correctly?

Mahika said, "It's time to eat Toby."

Let's run over Ted and return the ball to Justin.

Firefighters like superheroes save lives.

My hair like bananas is bright yellow.

Place your sticker here

Apostrophes

Some words can be combined to make a single, shorter word. These are contractions. Apostrophes show where letters have been removed.

For example:
The **gift is** wrapped. ▶ The **gift's** wrapped.
That **dog has** got our ball. ▶ That **dog's** got our ball.

Here are the verbs that are used most often in contractions. The letters in **bold** are those that the apostrophe replaces.

a**re**   a**m**   **is**   **would**   **will**   h**ave**   h**ad**   h**as**

Complete each sentence using the correct contraction.

We............painting a picture.   They............rather climb trees.

She............learning karate.   I............walk my dog later.

We often add 'not' to a verb to make a negative. Notice how there is no space between *is* and *not* in the final word.

For example:
is not ▶ isn't

Try to write these contractions. The first one has been done for you.

could not ......**couldn't**......

must not ....

have not ....

Tip: Some words don't follow the pattern.
will not ▶ won't
can not ▶ can't

Place your sticker here

Possessive apostrophes

An **apostrophe** can also show us that something belongs to someone.

The boy's bicycle.
The apostrophe before the **'s'** shows that the bicycle belongs to the boy.

Which of these phrases needs an apostrophe? Add apostrophes where you think they should go.

Mr Palmers house

The neighbours cat

Mums new car

The spring flowers

The dogs tail

This girls book

The ripe apples

The farmers field

When something is owned by more than one person or thing, the apostrophe goes after the 's' on the plural noun.

The boys' bicycles.
The bicycles belong to the boys.

But there are some exceptions. Not all plurals end in 's'.

The children's bunk bed
The bunk bed belongs to the children.

Tip: It's = it has or it is
Pronouns don't use apostrophes
The dog lost it's toy. ✗
The dog lost its toy. ✓
The dog lost its toy. It's really sad. ✓

Place your sticker here

Practising paragraphs

To help make our writing clear, it is split into paragraphs. There's a **Tip-Top** way to remember when to start a new paragraph.

TIP-TOP tip!

Time
When the time changes in your writing.
Two hours later
Three years before

Place
When the action moves to a new place.
In the attic
Over at Ted's house

Topic
When you write about a new subject, idea or theme. (More often used in non-fiction writing.)
Who was Shakespeare
What he did

Person
Each time a new person speaks.
"Good morning," said Tim.
"Is it?" replied Sam.
"Cheer up," said Tim.

Can you mark Jasmine's story with // each time a new paragraph should begin? The first one has been done for you.

The gingerbread man jumped from the oven onto the kitchen floor and ran away.// Out in the field he met a horse. "Hello," said the horse. Licking his lips, he began to chase the gingerbread man. "Run, run as fast as you can! You can't catch me. I'm the Gingerbread Man!" said the gingerbread man as he escaped. Later that day, as the gingerbread man was trying to cross a deep, fast river, he met a fox.

Place your sticker here

My handy grammar guide

Simple sentence

Independent clause

The race began.

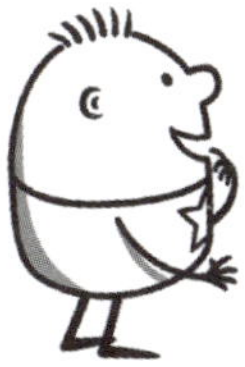

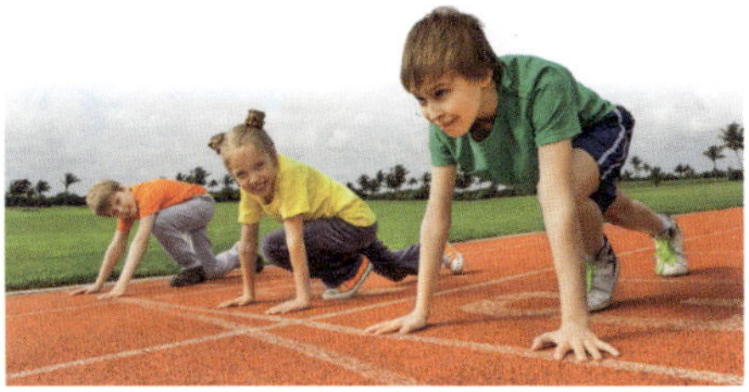

Compound sentence

Independent clause: Ada ran quickly

and

Independent clause: her friends cheered.

Complex sentence

Dependent clause: Until she received the gold medal,

Independent clause: she couldn't believe she had won.

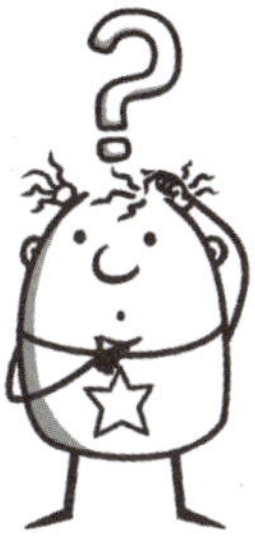

Determiner
A word that tells us if a noun is specific or general.

Adjective
Describes a noun.

Noun
A naming word for an object, person or place.

Modal verb
(Bossy verbs)
Show permission, ability or certainty of a verb.

Verb
Doing or being words. Verbs use tenses.

Adverb
Gives more information about a verb.

Preposition
Describes when or where something is or happened.

Pronoun
Can replace a noun.

Coordinating conjunction
Links two words or phrases as an equal pair.

Subordinating conjunction
Introduces a subordinate (dependent) clause.

Place your sticker here

Answers

✗ Pink for *think*. ✓ Green for *great*!

Naming nouns

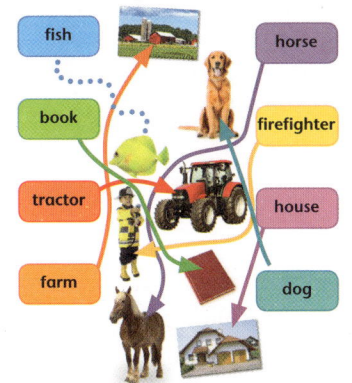

Capital letters and full stops
I have **a p**et hamster called **S**queak**.**
My **c**ousin **R**yan lives in **C**anada**.**
Daisy and **Z**oe are going to a **p**arty **o**n **S**aturday**.**
I'm **l**earning to **p**lay the guitar**.**

Muddled senteces
I have lots of friends.
I like playing football.
My dog is called Bobby.
I don't like getting up in the morning.
My birthday is in April.

Determiners
the zoo   **Which** monkey
those monkeys   **This** monkey
the tree   **that** monkey
One monkey   **some** grapes
my banana

an elephant   **an** orange
an aeroplane   **an** hour
a dragon   **a** house
an eagle   **a** unicorn

Adding adjectives
A **blue** / yellow fish
A **stripy** / spotty ball
A green / **red** apple
A slow / **fast** car
A **little** / big dog
A **tall** / short sunflower

Choosing adjectives
delicious meal   difficult sum
sandy beach   blue sky
fun party   tall tree

Expanding noun phrases
Examples of the sort of phrases you may have written:

A **red** umbrella.
An **unusual, red** umbrella.
An **unusual, red** umbrella **with black spots.**

Vital verbs
plays   clapped
jumps   drew

Past tense verbs
I <u>climbed</u> up a steep mountain last week.

I <u>played</u> tennis with my friends every day last week.

Last year, I <u>acted</u> in the school play.

Yesterday, I <u>finished</u> my homework then <u>watched</u> TV.

More past tense verbs
cry/cried   draw/drew
swim/swam   write/wrote
think/thought   see/saw
buy/bought   catch/caught
go/went   stand/stood

Using adverbs
I ran (faster). My heart beat (rapidly). The others were (quickly) catching up. As I crossed (over) the finish line, the crowd cheered (wildly). I (proudly) took first place.

The mouse ran **away** from the cat.
The children shouted **loudly**.
He arrived **early** at school.
I will **probably** go to the party.
She **always** danced when she was happy.

Word beginnings
unwell   **un**tidy
unload   **dis**like
unwrap   **re**fill

Word families
The *painter* **painted** the house.
The **driver** *drove* the bus.
The **climber** is *climbing* a mountain.
The *teacher* is **teaching** her class.
I **used** the eraser, but it was *useless*.
The **actor** is *acting* in a play.

Prepositions
She played **on** the swings.
May is **between** April and June.
We jumped **into** the puddle.
I will read **until** it's time for bed.

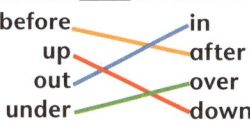

Personal Pronouns
I saw Jack today. **I** invited **him** to my party. I hope **he** can come. Amy is invited too, but it is **her** sister's birthday on the same day. Do you think **she** will come? I didn't tell either of **them** about the magic show. **It** will be awesome. **They** will love it.

Possessive pronouns
My team is in red and **hers** is in blue.

His dog is a terrier and **mine** is a poodle.

My favourite number is 5. What's **yours**?

Our t-shirts are the same, but **theirs** are different.

Their team lost and **our** team won.

I've got my ticket. Have you got **yours**?

Answers

✗ Pink for *think*. ✓ Green for *great*!

Helping verbs
The parrot ~~is~~/**are** squawking.
The balloons ~~is~~/**are** floating.
We ~~was~~/**were** jumping.
They ~~was~~/**were** swimming.
She **was**/~~were~~ eating.
The children ~~is~~/**are** playing.
The sheep ~~was~~/**were** in their field.
The fish **is**/~~are~~ swimming in its tank.

Making a sentence
Many dinosaurs **ate** only plants. ✓

Tyrannosaurus rex **had** a massive bite. ✓

Some of the biggest dinosaurs **had** the smallest brains. ✓

Compound sentences
I ate too much ice cream **and** I felt sick.

She wanted to say hello **but** she was too nervous.

I sprained my elbow **so** my arm was put in a sling.

You can either go to the pool **or** the cinema.

Fish have neither feet **nor** hands.

He dislikes the sand **yet** he is at the beach.

Short and sweet
Dear Ollie,
We are having a great time in Silver Bay. The weather has been hot and sunny every day. We went to the beach yesterday. Charlie and I had a surfing lesson. It was awesome. I hope you are enjoying your holiday. See you back at school next week.
Emily x

Complex sentences
You may have written the main clause or subordinate clause first.

I must brush my teeth **before I go to bed**.
Before I go to bed, I must brush my teeth.
Some parrots can talk **if you teach them**.
If you teach them, some parrots can talk.
Because I was cold, I wore my coat.
I wore my coat **because I was cold**.
I saw a lion **when I went to the zoo**.
When I went to the zoo, I saw a lion.
I feel so strong **since I took up karate**.
Since I took up karate, I feel so strong.

Sentence functions
C Take the dog for a walk.
E How marvellous!
Q Where do you live?
C Please post the letter.
S My birthday is next month.
E What beautiful birds!
S You're my best friend.
Q Will you tidy your room, please?

Using speech marks
"I can't. I've hurt my finger," replied Omar.
He showed Jess the plaster covering his finger.
"How did you do that?" asked Jess.
"A monster bit me the last time I played!" replied Omar.
"Ha, ha! Very funny!" laughed Jess.

Using commas
It was a warm**,** sunny day. Mum asked Connor to go to buy jam**,** flour**,** butter and eggs so that they could make a delicious cake for Grandma. Connor wondered if he should cycle**,** walk or run through the dark**,** spooky forest to get to the shops.

Commas for sense
Mahika said, "It's time to eat**,** Toby."
Let's run over**,** Ted**,** and return the ball to Justin.
Firefighters**,** like superheroes**,** save lives.
My hair**,** like bananas**,** is bright yellow.

Apostrophes
We**'re** painting a picture.
She**'s** learning karate.
They**'d** rather climb trees.
I**'ll** walk my dog later.

must not ▸ **mustn't**
have not ▸ **haven't**

Possessive apostrophes
Mr Palmer**'s** house
The neighbour**'s** cat
Mum**'s** new car
The spring flowers
The dog**'s** tail
This girl**'s** book
The ripe apples
The farmer**'s** field

Practising paragraphs
The gingerbread man jumped from the oven onto the kitchen floor and ran away.
⁋ Out in the field he met a horse.
"Hello," said the horse. Licking his lips, he began to chase the gingerbread man.
⁋ "Run, run as fast as you can! You can't catch me. I'm the Gingerbread Man!" said the gingerbread man as he escaped.
⁋ Later that day, as the gingerbread man was trying to cross a deep, fast river, he met a fox.